KENTE COLORS

KENTE COLORS

DEBBI CHOCOLATE

ILLUSTRATIONS BY JOHN WARD

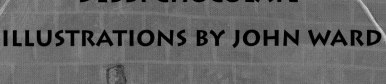

WALKER AND COMPANY
NEW YORK

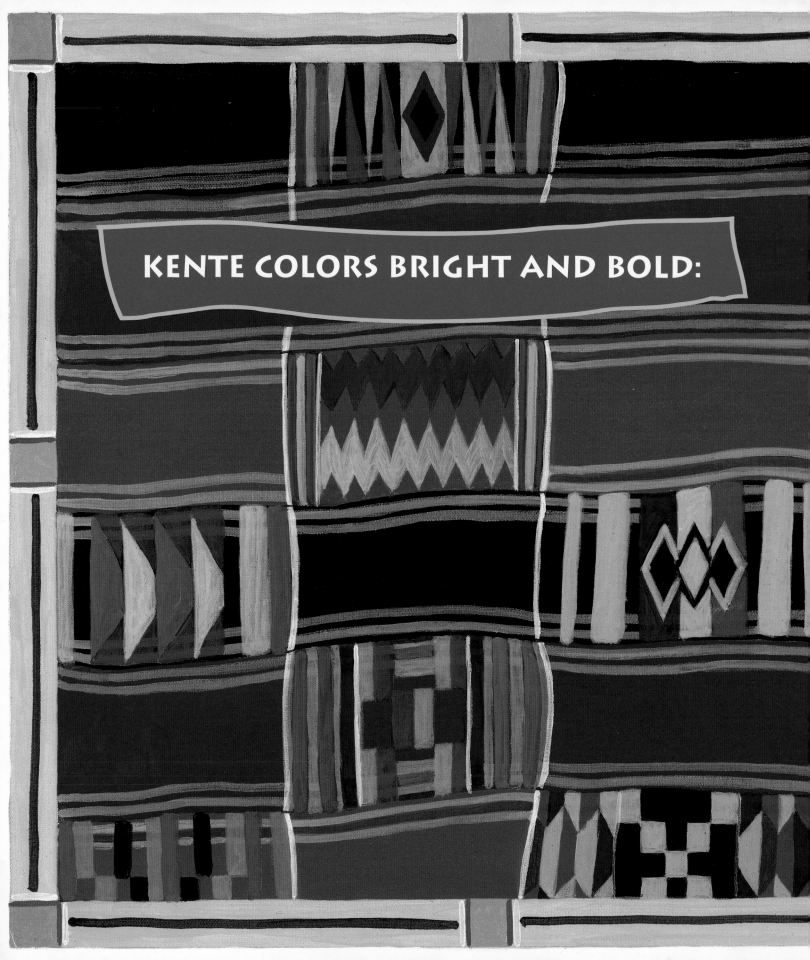

KENTE COLORS BRIGHT AND BOLD:

EMERALD KENTE FOR HARVEST TIME.

INDIGO BLUE FOR AFRICAN SKIES.

YELLOW KENTE FOR PINEAPPLES SWEET.

SUNSET KENTE RED AND DEEP.

MUD PIE KENTE RICH AND BROWN.

GOLD DUST IN A KENTE CROWN.

KENTE COLORS SILVER AND BLACK,
SWIRLING AROUND DANCERS' BACKS.

IVORY KENTE FOR DARK YOUNG BRIDES.

KENTE FOR A NEWBORN CHILD.

KENTE COLORS IN BRIGHT SILK ROBES—

FOR GENERATIONS YOUNG AND OLD.

Dazzling, colorful kente cloth made by the Ashanti people of Ghana and the Ewe of Ghana and Togo was once known as the cloth of kings. Four hundred years ago, at the height of the Ashanti Kingdom, only royalty wore kente. The word "kente" means "that which will not tear away under any conditions." Today, for all people of Ghana, traditional kente cloth is the national costume. It is often worn for ceremonial occasions: for festivals, weddings, and births.

In the weaving of kente cloth, cotton or silk kente strips are handwoven on narrow looms, then cut and sewn together side by side. Among the Ashanti and Ewe, the art of weaving kente is passed down from generation to generation.

Each pattern is produced by the placement of colors. Each patchwork of colors has a different meaning. "Gold dust," a mostly yellow pattern, symbolizes wealth and royalty. Another pattern, called "a wise old woman," symbolizes old age and wisdom. One pattern, called "that which has never happened before," symbolizes uniqueness. Many of the design names have historical references and have helped preserve Ashanti history. Some of the designs are proverbs and others indicate clan or status.

Colors are used symbolically in kente: green symbolizes bountiful harvest; blue represents love; ivory represents joy. Ghanaian men drape kente cloth over themselves and women wear kente as skirts, blouses, and matching headwraps. No matter how it is worn, kente cloth is an art form that is beautiful to behold.

FOR THE CHILDREN.
—D. C.

TO THE MEMORY OF MY MOTHER,
DIANNE ELIZABETH WARD.
I MISS HER SO MUCH.
—J. W.

First published in the United States of America in 1996 by Walker Publishing Company, Inc.

Published simultaneously in Canada by Thomas Allen & Son Canada, Limited, Markham, Ontario

Library of Congress Cataloging-in-Publication Data
Chocolate, Deborah M. Newton
Kente colors / Debbi Chocolate ; illustrations by John Ward.
p. cm.
Summary: A rhyming description of the kente cloth costumes of the Ashanti and Ewe people of Ghana
and a portrayal of the symbolic colors and patterns.
ISBN 0-8027-8388-0 (hardcover). —ISBN 0-8027-8389-9 (reinforced)
1. Ashanti (African people)—Costume—Juvenile literature. 2. Ewe (African people)—Costume—Juvenile literature. 3. Kente
cloth—Ghana—Juvenile literature. 4. Costume—Ghana—Symbolic aspects—Juvenile literature. [1. Ashanti (African people)—
Social life and customs. 2. Ewe (African people)—Social life and customs. 3. Kente cloth. 4. Ghana—social life and customs.]
I. Ward, John (John Clarence), ill. II. Title.
DT507.C48 1996
391'.0089'963374—dc20   95-23505
CIP
AC

Book design by Marva J. Martin

Printed in Hong Kong

2 4 6 8 10 9 7 5 3 1